Introducing Life

By Diana Kurniawan, MPH

Illustrated by: Ronald Kurniawan, BA

1663 Liberty Drive, Suite 200
Bloomington, Indiana 47403
(800) 839-8640
www.AuthorHouse.com

This book is a work of fiction. People, places, events, and situations are the product of the author's imagination. Any resemblance to actual persons, living or dead, or historical events, is purely coincidental.

First published by AuthorHouse 10/10/05

ISBN: 1-4208-6216-2 (sc)

Library of Congress Cataloging - In Publication Data.

Printed in the United States of America
Bloomington, Indiana

This book is printed on acid-free paper.

Warning:

This book contains some highly developed contents in life. It is fiction, … but not really, because the events described here, are conducive to heat; and often, limited to idealistic values of life, in a vacuum. If you don't really care, then it works, and this book is about a game, on who can finish first. How can you read, when you can't write, and how can you write, when you can't read? If there are some things you found useful in this book, *for your own life*, then write it down! If you don't find anything important at all, in this book; then you should read it again. It is not about the life that you lead, it is about, *how* you lead your life.

Table of Contents

A Little Prayer, for a Little Girl

By Diana Kurniawan

The doctor told me, she has a little heart, Lord
That's fine with me, Lord
But please let her grow up, to have a compassionate one.

The doctor told me, she will not be a smart one, Lord
That's fine with me, Lord
But please let her grow up, to be sweet and kind.

The doctor told me, she may loose her sight, Lord
That's fine with me, Lord
But please let her grow up, with a good voice to praise, You.

The doctor told me, she may not look normal, Lord
That's fine with me, Lord
I would rather have a daughter with character.

The doctor told me, she will have brittle bones, Lord
That's not fine with me, Lord
Because she is stronger than they think, Lord!

Please Lord, I will pray day and night, just don't let her die.
I love her, with all my unconditional love,
Please don't take my Sun away from me.

Introducing Life

Fiction by Diana Kurniawan

Birth, squirts of reddish particles, bubbled through this ligated, tubal path, in front of my paws, is it hands??? I have appendages, I have things, on my palms. There are some soft, brown, things, in between my fingers; protruding on each side, is a big finger, possible thumbs? Is this what a hand means to me? Always with something in between it, perhaps something Jewy (juicy, and gewy). Is there a light, at the end of this tube? Is this life? What is this life? It is full of sticky moments, and there are irrigations of blood, in the middle of my scream. I cannot hear myself, I am opening my mouth, the long food chain is gone! Where is the food tube? Is my mother a big world? Am I going to be in a different planet? Are there soft foods involved? I cannot live without those green things, the food tube likes to give me. It is alien, what is this red stuff? Is this my master? Is the master of the universe, at the end of this path? The force, pushes me forward. The bubbly stuff, arose again!! I am scared, there is a strange thing in front of me, an opening, a round opening, it is brown too!! It is open, and closed, it opens, and closed, it is inconsistent. What is this I am about to come and see? And the force still pushes. Please stop, I am not ready. I am not going to forget you food tube!!! Please let me go, please voice …please voice, let the forces stop; there is ordinary life, in here. I love it here, it is protected, I am encased in love. Is there love out there too? I do not know anything else, is my future bright? Is there a food tube there? How am I going to play with the voices, and the reddish particles stuff? Is there a way out? Am I the one, big, monster? Or does the voice, just talks to me? Can you bring me up, to the Lord?? Please, save a space for me!! No … please, whoaaaaaaaaaaaaaa!!!!! EEEE EEEEEEEEEeeeeeeeeeekKKKKKK!!!!

YEEEEKKKKKKKK! AAAAAAAAAAaaaaaaamamAaaaaaaar rrgghhhhhHH!

Stop hitting me!!!!

Weaeeeaaaaaaaaaaaaaa! Bleaaaaaaaaaaakkkkkkkkkaaaaaaaaaaa aaa!!! I am sad!!!!!!

Please forces, stop me, from going into the light … it is too bright!! It is too much!!!

I cannot handle it, please NO!!!!! How irate this makes me feel!! There is wind!! There are no such lovely things!! I see others, no wings, no more!!

Where is the music? And wings?? There are no such things…I cannot!! Please!!!

How come I cannot have my wings???!!!! Please, don't take that from me, it is the beauty of me. I am beauty!!!! I do not want to go, God!!!! Don't leave me!!!! I am not ready!!!!!!

Come back!!!!!!!!!!

Sperm

Clubbin' in Homeland

Fiction by Diana Kurniawan

"You're like a baby on crack! Remember what your mama taught you! Don't forget!" I said with force, and a little beguiled timidity. I said that, after he said, "Baby, you're hot!!! Do you wanna sex me up?" A girl must be clever these days, no matter how old or young we are, women are targets. The seduction of mankind in sex, or shall we say "making love," has become a regular norm, in inner cities youth. I am so upset, because I am surrounded with cases of teenage pregnancy, and divorce survivors. "At least I made it" said one of them. "Yeah right, you know they had to go through some suicidal thoughts!" said another. This is the true nature of some.

Does that seem a little familiar? Is our generation X,Y, Z and the rest of the alphabets, starting over again without an alpha, a beginning? Is there an end, to these dilemmas of sex, with too much casualties left behind, and dreams tattered? It was supposed to be easy … you go to the egg, and fertilize. You are born, mommy and daddy comes, to hold *you*; then, school starts, and you have friends.

Perhaps, a girlfriend, or a boyfriend, and you study. No drugs, no brutality, no sex to ruin your dreams, or even domestic violence, to start ruining your situations. This is what life is supposed to be like for kids, simple, and kind. Then war breaks out, either at school, or at home, or between America, and Iraq! Spilt milk, lack of tolerance, lack of honesty, lack of sexual knowledge, lack of money, it was powerful!! How did it all begin? There was a force somewhere there...I couldn't find out. I bet Satan did it!!

Comes the dating world ... it's a competition now. It is strictly survival of the fittest, and there is no room for second best. Everyone is out to compete, for the finest, cutest, successful, sweetest man, ever, alive! Women are in competition. The ration is getting smaller, and there are lack of providers, of love. There are not a lot of women, with enough chances; and there are not a lot of sharing of goodness around, instead, a lot of cheating going on. The men have won. There is a male to female ratio competition, ladies. I am on the lead. You want to follow? You want to work hard, and get your man? Is that the trouble we are facing today? Women are not getting married, and have too much pressure to be a wife, mother, and lover? Then we must be good. I think, there was too much experimentation going on. I wonder whom? I admit, I didn't understand the power of sex. Did you?

Sex: everyone wants some, but does that mean we must abuse it, and think, "I will no longer be a virgin, otherwise, guys won't like me; and they will have too much pressure, or I am too inexperienced?"

I was, at one time, a perfect chicá from the East-Los part, of the Southern California, Angeles. I reside as an immigrant, student, as well as daughter, below the federal poverty level. I too, felt the failures of love, and pains of social class, meets prince charming...I felt it doesn't exist. I understand, it was difficult, for a long time ...

All through the periods in our years, we have a common bond, that is to be loved. Now, women must work for that love, and now; working, is part of the necessity. These days, our challenge to know the issues to vote, is combined with the pressure of being successful, and rich. Information is key, access is glory. We've been working for it, or pray to be "lucky." Do you have the time? When you are feeding a baby? Or working at Sav-On, to pay for your daughter's dream, of becoming a singer? Then come home, to help your family? Everyone has to be taken care of...so now it's our turn. There is hope, if rapists can rape, then we can have our chance of true love. It is not a crime. We can do it. It has been proven, love does exist. Don't ask me to arrange it, know yourself, if it's right, you can feel it.

Don't go knockin' on heaven's door, wait your turn! Is there a surge, outlet of electricity, when you see him? Then fight, not hurt; and it does matter, how he treats you. Since I am weak, a pretty girl, with a little attitude, and personality adjustment problem; but seem to know the difference, between friend, or foe. I have seen the worst, even criminals. Bad men must stop. Cheating, beating, extra-marital affairs, and divorces are unkind. I had no hope, violence hit me. You can do it though, I'm in the process; like a tire, I am relentless. Just hold on a little bit more, there is fun to await, whether with friends, or mankind. Know where your family is, your issues, *your* love, and be strong.

Pandora's box had been opened, and my father's daughter, just went clubbin'.

Bondage

Fiction by Diana Kurniawan

I sat in my uncle's condo, whilst on his couch, the telephone rang; the devil is here, my voice in my thought answered. I saw a praying hand, as if God's presence is in the air, and I saw the glittering light, while my head spins like a headache on that couch. He asked me, "why are you so hard to put up with? I am easy, my yolk is hard." Then I replied, "You are hard, my yolk is easy, and I am not an egg. This is the beginning of a good friendship." I enthralled him, my Buddhist ex-boyfriend, who believed in Agnosticism. "I do not condemn you, but I am sure Christianity plays a role in my marriage, so he has to listen!"

Look!!! A sower went out to sow. And as he sowed, some seeds fell along the path, and the birds came, and devoured it. Other seeds, fell on rocky ground, where it had not much soil, and immediately, it sprang up. Since it had no root, it withered away; when the sun rose, it was scorched, and since it had no root, it withered away. Other seeds, fell among thorns, and the thorns grew up, and choked it, and it yielded no grain. And other seeds fell into good soil, and brought forth grain; growing up, and increasing, and yielding thirty fold, and sixty fold, and a hundred fold. Mark 4: 3-8. I am a rose, amongst the thorns, for the thorns had given me beauty. I am of a different seed, the new kind. It is not good, from my experience, to sow seeds in other people's heads to manipulate *their* believes. *Do not harm them, just inform*, that the world exists, and the higher power reigns.

I was not sure, if his marriage will work with mine; it is ideal in my mind, but not in others. Is it my fault? *Not to harm you, but to inform you*, that I am a dweller in the cave of this world, but bats around me transformed into Dracula, to suck my sexual desire, then abused it, in the house of the Lord? My uncle was upset that Nasty Boy, and I, had oral sex, in His dwelling. The scary thing was, I did not tell my uncle, and neither did my ex-boyfriend, *I hope.*

I defied God, once and for all. He showed His hand, is upon me, and reminded me of the soft ground, we are in. "You have let satan in His house," the voice in my mind, and heart replied. I am not to mix my religion, if I am uncertain, and he is not a believer. Foundation has to be soiled. I am un-experienced, "know your Bible well," the Lord, answered. Nasty Boy is evil in the mind, good in hands, but took it out, on the wrong person. Be aware of the devil, and his existence, his name shall be proclaimed. FIGHT BACK!!! I am ashamed of myself.

I hope that he only told, only *one*, of his many friends, about our sexual relationship. I thought it was safe, just like the mutual masturbation episode, most high schoolers do…but this time, I know it's more than that. There were more words involved, than love. I have been bondaged, by domestic violence, and abuse, and the perpetrator, was my own lover. What ever happened to the girl, and boy, love story? No one told me about the heat…sex, yes; the heat was never something we discussed. I was bondaged by love, for one another, but is that my fault? Can I be a Christian, with love for this atheist? Agnostic? Maybe he was that kid, in people's emails, of how he walked home, while contemplating suicide? Can I love, a suicidal man? Can anyone love me, after this domestic violence? Maybe, my uncle heard from someone? How? Was that the phone call he just had?

Possible psychotherapy…again.

How You Doin'?

Fiction by Diana Kurniawan

How does it feel to be a pretty girl, with jealousy in her heart?

There is always a reason to sabotage her. Her dress is too cute, her accent is enticing, her hair is too pretty, her eyes, too seductive. Her ar*e well endowed, that allows my ex-boyfriend, to break up with me. Is it *me*? Or is it her? Is it *him*? Who wants to feel wanted, and her heart is too good, that makes *him*, compare me? Is it *her* fault? She was born to be a super-star?

Seductive goddess, luscious queen???

Her awesome-ness, grace, and wit too strong, and full of intelligence, that genius CFO's (that's Chief Financial Officers … to you) turn around, to meet, and greed her hands with kisses, coming down from mankind? She is heavenly, is this you?

Have you felt this way? Or did she ever back stab you, at one time, because he became interested in her, not you anymore, anytime, since you did not give him the time? Is this you? Is your name B*@$H ?!?!?!!?!

Witch?? Or plain' ol cheerleader, wannabe?

This is high school for you, isn't?

This is college for life, for me!! The strong survives, and the brainiacs think!

I am ready for marriage, baby!!! Are you? Or are you just ready, to harass me?

Then afterwards, you tell me, HAH . . . I HAVE A BOYFRIEND!!! Nice! ☺ I hope he screws on you, and die!

There are plenty women, with degrees, extra-curricular activities, and still have no ends, in meeting the right man. Is this why Public Health women have been single? Are these the choices, they have to live with? Be single, for the rest of your life, because you are married to the job? Is this just negativity talking, or is there an end to this? The men stay strong, and at times, even have subtle harassment techniques; so sly, that even the doves can't see. "Women stick together," said some men, not anymore my friends. Now we have too many, and it has been a crowd, that over population, creates a disease.

Claustrophobia of the female species, there are too many of me around, and so little time. I am getting older, and time is getting younger. There are longer life expectancies, with being alone. Now, the young, gets the gold; and the cheated upon, gets the left-over. This is Sylvia Plath talking, her memory cannot be erased, she cannot divorce, again!! Not from her mind, nor her ambition, and especially, not from her husband. I am sorry sweetie, her dream is still alive, and I wish, so too, are her children's. The temptation never ends … it's okay to be me.

Is it my fault, I'm just different? Why sabotage?? Just carry a gun!!!

Or protect yourselves, from criminals, instead of me. Why are you so afraid, of competition? That you have to hurt your competitor? Is it because … I have talent? Or money? Or nice car? Or nice body? Or just nice?

Is it me?

Are you a friend, friend? Is this how you, perceive me, to be?

A girl, whom you love to punch in the face? Spat upon, die on the crucifixion gathering, stabbed on her side, bleeding to death; while crowned with a crown of thorns, from the roses I received, from a guy you've liked? Is it okay for me, to like a White guy? While I'm Chinese, Indonesian, and Presbyterian??? Why do I still feel like an outcast, or just dying, for acceptance from you? Do you feel like God? Does it help you? Because it hurts me. I am sorry … I am sorry to be me. Will you like me, if I commit suicide??

Perhaps you will frame me??? There are girls, women, princesses; who can feel, and yes, absolutely … movie stars indeed. Is that how you see me? Respect me. I think that's what happened, when you succeed, people like me, become a game. I feel me, and

I don't want success; I want to be gay, and happy!!! Too bad, that's not meant for me!

I want to be loved, and I want people to love me!!! Sylvia Plath was me, and the advantages, are more than what you see. Please see me, I am dying, … and let the dying breed stay!

There is a need for diversity, there is a need, for me. Should women think once again, of the consequences they have placed on one another? Could you just be yourself these days? Or is this the weakness in me? The strong survives, and there is no guilt in criminality. Competition is getting stronger, and traditional women, are getting weaker. Where does that fit me?

p.s.: don't hurt the interns, teach them well.

Salma's Gun

Desperation in the Flesh

Fiction by Diana Kurniawan

Desperation in the flesh:

I CANNOT control myself anymore … (crying profusely) … I cannot help it, and I cannot forgive myself … perhaps I shouldn't have loved, but it was not a mistake to love, is it? I just wanted to love him.

Good Person #2:

It is never a mistake to love, but it's definitely hard to find love in the *right* person.

Desperation in the flesh:

I thought he was the right person. There was a moment in the café, when we were in our University commons area. We stared into each other's eyes, and I was so scared, that I left. I was not single at the time, so I waited, until I was confident enough to do so.

Good Person #2:

Then why did you ask him out?? So far later in life, 2 years later? That was too long, and besides, that was *his* job, to ask a girl for dinner.

Desperation in the flesh:

I was infatuated, I couldn't stop thinking of him … I was not sure, if I will ever find him again, for the rest of my life. It took me 2 years, to make sure I should do it.

Good Person #2:

Are you sure that was it … or was it just a serendipitous thought, that you put into action; and mistakenly, conceive it to be a destined mistake?

Desperation in the flesh:

I was not sure … I was sure of my feelings, and I thought that it would not hurt; to be the lovely woman that I am.

Good Person #2:

Then what happened?

Desperation in the flesh:

I called his house, talked to his mom, to ask him out to dinner.

Good Person #2:

Yes, you asked a man to dinner! Then what happened?

Desperation in the flesh:

I was his prostitute in the raw, we became sexually active. He was not respectful towards me, after we became intimate. He wanted me, to be his *one-night-stand.*

Good Person #2:

It was not your fault, I've heard this before … but why did you let him? To such *things*? If you didn't want to sleep with him, then why did you sleep with him?

Desperation in the flesh:

I was desperate, I was so infatuated, that I thought the best thing to do, was follow this passion. Take my control, to claim love, instead of ***regret*** for life. I didn't know that I will eventually end with the same outcome ... *regret for life.*

Good Person #2:

I am very sorry for you. I wish you had not slept with him. Was this the *crack* that turned the code?

Desperation in the flesh:

What do you mean?

Good Person #2:

The girls that you are worried about. The ones, whom you believe will marry him in the future .. whom? How did they come about?

Desperation in the flesh:

I knew them from school, and they somehow knew that he was good looking, and they asked me if I had known him.

Okay, let me take that back. I actually told them about him, because I didn't know who else to turn to. I needed a friend, and I told them since, I knew Tiffany from University, and I knew Elizabeth, since high school, the same with "Masturbator" and "Juanita". They don't know him, but they were my friends.

Good Person #2:

What have they done to you??

Desperation in the flesh:

They grilled me. Tiffany set me up with a Korean Gangster to be "vultured" upon, and she wanted Christian, to herself.

The same with Elizabeth, because they both believe, that with me, dead, or suicidal; they can claim victory, to win a husband! Christian!! I think Elizabeth, actually KILLED A GIRL FROM MY SCHOOL!!!!

Good Person #2:

So they **STALKED** you, and **USED** you as a meat market. So they can kill you, for the money, and win him as a prize? Is he famous or something??

Desperation in the flesh:

They said, "it's all fair in love, and war." Tiffany and Elizabeth are the same person, except different in culture, race, tradition, and everything opposite to me. Do you think they will do that? Do you think they will marry him? Or do you think one of them will marry Christian? I was the only one, who believed in true love, while Tiffany and Elizabeth, believed in: grotesque survival competition.

Is this how *it is* in the world? Is this what it is like in the world? My life turned into a mockery, and spied for access to cute men, so other women can use me, then eventually stab me ... to be killed by more people in the future???!!! Please friend ...is this true?

Good Person #2:

Is he famous? Rich?? Handsome, as the Devil?

Desperation in the flesh:

Yes, or something like that ... he is an athlete in University, and still is, I believe. I know that he knows someone in Hollywood. I never told anyone, anything; until I was so desperate in sadness, and needed a friend. I was not aware of their cunning ways, and I thought, I could let off some steam, to give out my reckless past.

I didn't know (crying .... crying ....crying).

Good Person #2:

He was a liar. He shouldn't have done those things to you. If he does marry one of them, your friends, then you can use the ***State Penal Code for stalking and abuse***. They have no idea who he is, ***unless through you, especially if they are***

<u>from different walks in your life.</u> They are criminals, and you don't need to worry about that.

Desperation in the flesh:

I am very sad, and scared, that I might be suicidal again. I am going to be suicidal, if they all met each other, date each other, and be married eventually. Please don't!!!!!

Good Person #2:

Read my lips sweets … ***<u>PENAL CODE!!!!</u>*** This is not right, they cannot stalk a woman, and steal her life, after she had been beaten by them!! This is called *blackmail, stalking, and can lead to murder*, and those crimes, are *liable by imprisonment.* Guilty Tiffany must have stalked you too, and him as well, to get through him, and you. Elizabeth definitely had stalked you, especially if she knew you, for the sake of meeting a man, *you* met first. Elizabeth will continue to do this, until she wins something out of you. Tell the COPS!!!!!!!! This jerk-off called "Christian" obviously has some knowledge of your past, because he wouldn't have met them, when he knew that you were hurt by him, officially termed, *stalking an ex-girlfriend.*

Desperation in the flesh:

WHY ME??????!!!! (crying) PLEASE!!!!! PLEASE STOP HATING ME!!!!! PLEASE!!!!!

(She cupped her ears, and cringing the strands of her hair)

Good Person #2:

Did Christian know them? Before he met you? Did you see any of them, meet with Christian?

Desperation in the flesh:

Yes, I saw Elizabeth, and Christian, met at Alhambra AMC Theatre. The sad thing was, I was to meet "Masturbator" there, and I saw Elizabeth talking to Christian there. My friend Sunny, told me about what Elizabeth had done. Sunny told me to go to the movie quickly, because he was scared of Elizabeth, since she betrayed me.

I was so sad, and I started to cry … it was not right … I was not to be treated this way. I did nothing wrong, to any of them.

I am not a criminal, or a looser, or a sad story of a life, to be written everywhere, and hurt more by them.

I cannot let them do this, please help me. I don't know what to do. I am so hurt… (crying…crying…contemplating suicide).

Good Person #2:

How about Tiffany, she met him too???!!!!

Desperation in the flesh:

She set me up with a Korean Gangster, who hurt me, more than anyone in the world could do. It was a crime, friend. I reported, and I reported, and I will continue to report. It was ***NOT*** my fault … please understand.

Good Person #2:

How did you know of him, this Christian? How did you know where to find him anyhow?

Desperation in the flesh:

I was watched by him, he kept LOOKING at me, as if he knew, who I was. I didn't know how he knew of me, or how he noticed me. There was this chemistry, and I was very scared of that. I waited, and made sure that I was single. At that time, I had a boyfriend. But later, two years down the line, I just followed a hunch of his name, and searched in the internet. I thought his name was Christian Jackson, it turned out, he's just Christian. I found out, he was a baseball star. That's what I meant by athlete.

Good Person #2:

He was trouble to begin with, most athletes can be. I am so sorry, and I hope you can gain solace from what you have gone through, by going to therapy. My dear, this is important ... hurt can turn into pain later, and if not taken care of .. deep depression. I am sorry to break it down to you.

Desperation in the flesh:

I wish he was not un-respectful, I wish all this, didn't happen. I wish he wouldn't have hurt me, so deeply. I wish he didn't meet *any* of the bad friends I had. I wish I can turn it all back. I was in love, with a bad person. I wish I can make sure, those friends that have hurt me, will never hurt me; and never try to kill me in the future. I wish Christian never existed.... I wish I can take it all back ... I wish ... I wish, please God, please help me (tears, are now fluids of frustration).

I wish he was not the one. This turned into love ... unattainable. I am sorry for this ... I cannot live like a vagrant, without direction, and love. I need you GOD!!! PLEASE HELP ME!!!! I wish I can turn back time (crying).

Good Person #2:

Sweets, you have gone through a crime....this is called, a crime. Please stop crying. It is best to let the authorities know about this. They may do something else to you in the future, and you need to get help. Sign up for counseling, and ask your counselor; perhaps for group therapy, where you will see people, who have gone through some other traumas in their lives. I am very sorry.

Desperation in the flesh:

Now I know why people commit suicide. I am so hurt, and in pain ... it hurts so much, I cannot bear the cost of this.

Good Person #2:

I am so sad, that he stalked you, and hurt you. I am sorry, did he say what he wanted from you, that he hurt you in that way?

Desperation in the flesh:

He was young, he said, …he said, he was young, and he just wanted what he can get…meaning sex, and I was so hurt by that. He said that the situation is the same, as getting a discount, at a restaurant. I was not sure why he wanted to meet the girls that went to high-school with me. Tiffany wanted to be a movie star, she was willing to kill me, to get to the top. Elizabeth, is beautiful, and a lawyer, she wanted to kill me, to get to the top as well. I was not sure why, **I** became a target, when I have told them both, that he had hurt me, *severely.* I was gearing towards my future; but they have taken so much time out of my life. They have taken so much time!!! It is so difficult, please God, please HELP ME!!! PLEASE!!!!!!!

Good Person #2:

They all wanted the same thing when they are young, sweets. They are all scared, and cannot face the facts, that they needed to change, and stop mocking other people's lives!! They all want to be the best, and they will try, EVERY way, to get there. This is serious sweets … I am scared for you.

Desperation in the flesh:

I am so scared that they will try to kill me, to have a happy life! It's not fair … please help me … please help me … I have been stabbed so many times, that I am so scared; that they will shoot me, anytime … to gain *everything* they wanted. They told me that I had pulled a "line," or that I'm "Passover."

Good Person #2:

They will continue to mock you, my dear. I will pray for you. I know that they must have mocked you, and your life. Don't think about them, if they are going to be friends, they are going to be friends; because of you, and the crime they committed. It is called, **BLOODY FRIENDSHIPS.** They will become criminals, all together, at the same time. Don't keep them in your mind, stay as far as possible; and they will die, in their own hell.

Desperation in the flesh:

I am immigrant. I am so scared that my cost of living in the United States, was to be robbed by criminals, so they can gain fame, happiness, and riches, when I was the one in love with him. I moved to this country, to have a better life, and I didn't know that they would have battered me, as food to be eaten, and thrown away as trash. I wish I never met any of them. I am scared, that I will be killed by them. I am scared that Elizabeth, and Tiffany, will eventually marry him. Then, purchase a gun to re-track their crimes.

Good Person #2:

I know how you feel, they have used you, and they invaded *your privacy.* I wish I knew them before, so I could stop them, where they were. This is not just your mistake, this is *their* crime. Please live *through* it, because you will eventually see their fruits; rotten, and sinister, to become their own knives, for their backs.

Desperation in the flesh:

What can I do now? I seldom speak to others, I became indigent. I was beaten by others, that I cannot concentrate, and have any freedom anymore. My immigrant experience, became a living joke to them (crying, profusely). I even thought Elizabeth will eventually kidnap my future.

Christian just wanted to have a beautiful, rich, and hypocritical wife, and end up stabbing me, on my back, because he can.

Good Person #2:

He may, or may not, want to use that opportunity; because there are so many single people in the world, that he does not need to hurt you more. Unless, he meant to kill your future.

He doesn't have the right to back stab you, in the way you have described; especially, if he is good looking, and he knows famous people. You stay with the Lord, and there is <u>*time*</u> on your side.

Desperation in the flesh:

His defenses was, "it is hard to meet good looking people, whom he is attracted to."

Good Person #2:

Then that's the time you need to speak to the local police, and write a report, on how Elizabeth, and Tiffany, both had followed you, to meet Christian, or meet his "Hollywood" friends. You can do the same to him, because you don't stalk him, to his apartment, or to meet his "baseball stars" friends.

Desperation in the flesh:

What should I do now? (crying) Please help me … Please …

Good Person #2:

You are not alone, you have God, and time, *on your side.* They have a crime in their past, please believe in yourself, and keep praying. Prayers will help you, in the long run.

<u>Promise to do something good with your life.</u> <u>Please don't think you will not be able to gain your future back.</u> Many famous people became solid role models, because they have gone through a major trauma, and have gained control in their lives. There are millions of people, whom you have not met. Christian does not need Elizabeth, because he has hurt you; and he will live with that mistake, in his future. Christian does not need Tiffany, for the same reason, and if they meet, they will meet because of a crime, and by hurting someone close to home. This matter is close to attempted murder.

"They can claim a good life, as they saunter in their yacht, but you have a clean history. God will be with you, He will never forsake you."

Repeat those words, inside your mind, as long as it takes to survive.

Desperation in the flesh:

"They can claim a good life, as they saunter in their yacht, but I will have a clean history, and God will be with me. He will never forsake me."

Good Person #2:

Don't let man hurt you anymore, they cannot hurt you anymore, choose life.

Desperation in the flesh:

I will choose life, dei gratia.

Compromise

Fiction by Diana Kurniawan

Have you ever wondered why I love you so much the way I do? The way I love you, is like any other, love is love. Yet, I will never know why, or how, I could be in such a state, heart break. I feel like pancake, on a platter with flowers on top, because you've created me on a pan, to be grilled, and fancied, to be devoured. I was battered, and I think you have taken the syrup out of my life. I can't seem to forget the past, my love for you, was everlasting.

I see your beauty, I see your grace, and action adventure, dramatic life, of a bachelor meets Prince Charming; but I can't seem to know, why I can't forget you?

I know, I am "damaged", I guess all girls have their flaws; be it domestic violence, hatred towards mankind, or just plain hate, or maybe revenge? Perhaps I should be vengeful, but I can't seem to know the difference, between me, and the rest of the other ladies. I can't seem to forget the past; my love for you, was everlasting.

I guess the low self-esteem you all mentioned to me, is also everlasting; like my love and my a*se. I now know, I am just a girl, with a lot of work to do, and a lot of running to attain. I have tried to do just a mile or two, then now, up to 2.4 miles for 40 minutes; and my arse still looks flabby. To think it all came from just one comment. "You have a big butt, I don't like the way you dress, you look like a grandma," was just uncalled for. It was a little harsh at first, but now that I think about it, it was gruesome. I think I would like to switch places now, maybe you'd like to be me for once. Maybe, we could start first with, hmm .... the stoning incident. Yes, I was a Christian needing attention, but I think Indonesia, gave me too much. Then there is the first kiss, by a guy who did not like me, because I did not have enough money, to be with him. Another of good looks, that women criticize me, then another, who saw me as trash. A cheater then came, a rapist next, a serial killer/con-artist, bi-sexual, anarchist, and finally, Italian mafia. I am starting to give up on you men, or actually, hate all of you. Is it because I was not good enough? I was clean when I first met you. Then everyone poked fun, and wanted me to be the last woman alive, to be married.

Is it my smile? Do I have crooked teeth, or hairy mole? Even if I do, does it matter to you? Can't you overlook my ugly, with my beauty? Or does my ugliness inside, scares you so much, that my eyes tear, with sadness, when I think of how beautiful you are? Am I just a joke? Is this *your* calling of me? I was supposed to be your wife. I wanted to get married, have children, beautiful kids, move out from our dumpy apartment, to a cute house. Then, live happily together, as a family. Was I going too fast for you?

Some girls are already preparing their stalking plans, and some of you, decided to stalk me, to get to them; but why? So I reported, your vision of a perfect wife, am I too harsh? Is loving me so different compared to others? What would you like me to do? Need I be a maid? A superstar? Glamour girl? Sexy Diva? Or can I have just what I have, and feel pretty? Can't you love me, just the way I love you? Why do you always compare? Why is it so hard for me, to be the right person? Can't I be marriage material too? Or at least, be a beautiful bride in your arms, because I think of you, as marriage material? Must there be cheating going on? Aren't there enough single women out there, already? I'm your queen, please treat me, as I should. I love me, can't you please love me too? I know it's not me, because I never thought it was you. There is always a wandering eye, perhaps that's why.

I am socially inadequate now, I kept getting abused, and being treated as meat, amongst you, vultures, or men. One of you said, "you should put acid in your eyes, then be blind. Maybe I'll marry you," as he kissed my neck, and slipped his hands, inside my panties. "You're a whore, might as well have sex with me, and marry me," then he inserted his index finger inside my vagina, without my permission. I am a joke to him.

"I'll make porridge out of you," as he continued to feed my brain, and my heart, with brutal words, of how I should not believe in God, instead believe in him. How my heart speaks louder than words, he does not seem to care to hear! I just want your attention, is that hard for you? To spend a little bit of your time, to speak with me, be my baby, and love me tenderly? Don't I deserve a loving man too? YES, I DO !!!!!

Is it because there are so many beautiful women out there? You want me to commit suicide? Why?? Why do you say that to me? Why are you so mean? Am I trash to you? I am not smart enough? ... Is that it? Why can't you be happy for me? It's not my fault, I was born mediocre. I am special that way.

I was not as clean, as I was before, can I still be with you? Or must there be a scale, I should know about? You thought I was crazy? I was crazy about you, now I am going crazy, because of you. So maybe we should talk, instead of you, comparing me to other people.

I've asked God for a good man, but most want me, to pamper them. Are you guys babies? Scratch my back, and I'll scratch yours. Do unto others, as you would do unto yourselves. I am so sad these days, men womanize, and ladies patronize, fellow women with courage to battle.

Women are getting angrier. There are some men, however, who act like women, and women like men. Are we forgetting our roles?

Are we acting silly again? Or is civil war going to happen for the second time, this time men vs. women. Are we trying to hard to save the world, that we have forgotten to save ourselves??

Are divorce rates climbing, AGAIN??? I think it's time to stop, but will you still take me, just the way I am?

Satanic Cho

Fiction by Diana Kurniawan

My hands grasping for air, heart traumatized, juggernaut inside my temples, conflict with my will. The wrinkles of my hyper-cerebellum, transferred to my laughing lines, and made it disappear. No laughs, no write, no poetry, just misfortune. Words of violence, retaliation, of how a person should write, or speak the heart, when the only thing I thought of throughout the day is … rape.

Do I deserve this? Is writing going to help me possess some qualities, or will difficulties dwell in my future, of my past?

I started to write about past history, my mouth dry from talking to myself, but I cannot place on paper, my hardships, and questions of why I became this way. It just happened. I trusted, and I could not write. The prose I've written, and pieces I represent, will no longer be the same. He took them. My future disappeared, with just a forceful kiss, mixes of sexual desire, and lack of timidity. He was brutal.

He could not tell me, why he did so, I told him, "I will report!!"

He said, "You don't have the slightest self-esteem!!!"

"Too late, El Segundo knows you," I clicked, hung-up, walked out of my mind, and tried to release the frustrated angst. It became hate, my heart, my soul, my love turned 180 degrees Fahrenheit, boiling, filled with bacteria, congested with diseases. Post-Trauma-Post-Rape-Post-Crying Sessions, my fingers seizures for air, as flashbacks continued, my head crying, "Oxygen me please!"

He first cupped my mouth, grabbed my chest, as I said, "I am not ready for this!" That was all the thoughts I had. I kept thinking, not writing. I am on drugs, probably now, I will always be. Continual frustration from his criminality transferred to me. Now I could write, no I can't, it's not right ... is retaliation through paper correct? But I've reported, case closed.

Could I have handled the situation differently? Yes, I was not supposed to be there. I asked for a ride, who knew she'd say, "too far."

My computer is my only friend, along with my Father, family, and at times... high school mates. This life? What am I supposed to say? I hate it.

Congratulations boyfriend, you've won. You were just an acquaintance, rapist at once!!! Could I write again? This time with flaw, full of symbolism of negativity, positivity taken out of me. Partly me, partly Satan, partly poetry, God HELP ME!!!

I could not talk, this is not right. There were people asleep, what about Shelley? Didn't she like you? Marina was the best in the East, pride of the West, why did you pick me? Please go, I should go, where was my key? Did you hide it from me? I hope you don't have HIV!!!

My brain popped that night, he pressured my mouth, with one hand, clenching both of mine; the other left hand, parting my thighs, which was closed tight at the knees. He grabbed, separated, parted the sea of my body, furthering my legs with his, and his mouth, quenched my oral cavity.

I could feel his jaw bone, skull to skull, I felt my brain popped, on the left side, the creative one. He thieved my soul; I tried to run, and he grabbed my spirit.

"If you unlock the door, I will kill you with this knife," he stood there. "Where did he get the knife?" I asked myself. This was planned? Why?

I was kind, my guard was down.

I was in the picture, framed. He wants my diary, my writing, he wants me, to write about him, then I would be free!!! But I could not write about him, I am struggling for air, I breathed through my nose. Like Mister Miyagisan told me, "wax on, wax off, …this time you're off!!!" He whispered. He knows kung-fu…but I don't know you! I thought in my head. I can't write!! I am not allowed to, he told me.

"Let the black people go first!! Let the Chinese, Korean, Japanese, White people, and Hawaiian go!!! You are last! And that's where you belong!!" He whispered, as he cupped my mouth. "I am not a good writer, and I am a singer, and I am part Chinese!" I cried inside, I could not say a thing. I was unsure, of what he was doing to me. My writing is twisted now, as he twists me around, and around merrily. "This is maneuver!" He told me. "Is this rape?" I thought….no it cannot. I am not a victim, just a person. I AM NOT!!!

I can't write my life on paper, because this happened, they will not love me. They will disrespect my whole entity!!!! What will I be? Could I write? Should I write?

The hardships, of a writer of violence.

I was once pretty.

Noise of Hate and Prejudice

Thursday

By Diana Kurniawan

I believe I am crazy, and I seem to not know, the reason why I feel that my boundaries of sanity, and insanity, has been broken down. Was I born with a genetic defect? Is this the PTSD talking? I am not depressed anymore, because the medication has helped me, in coping with the sadness, and negative thoughts. Yet, inside my heart, there is this strange feeling of illusion, and craziness … is it the Devil, or is this too much caffeine? I may sound humorous to some, but I have to assure myself, that I am *not* that bad, and *not* crazy. I can't wait to talk, to my psychiatrist, and tell him all of the details of my thoughts, and how I am not sure of my own psychological senses. It has gotten rotten, and my sane thoughts now, are not at all straight …

My sanity, convoluted, with ideas of how crazy, or mind boggling, I have become in the past few years. Five years to be exact, since I was first exposed to oral sex, by my ex-boyfriend, Mark. WITHOUT MY PERMISSION!!! Then in 2001, I was brutally raped by Satanic Cho … I am not coping as well as I have thought.

I am not at fault, am I?? Should I have driven, to go home? That night I was tipsy, and intoxicated? Yet, I felt very sexual, as my inhibition goes down, and Satanic Cho massaged my pubic region. Should I have ran? I was attracted to him, but I didn't know he was going to rape me. I am not a bad person, please God, please help me. I am not that bad of a person. I asked permission, afterwards to Shelley, because she was in love with Satanic Cho, and I was already raped (meaning I have slept with him, *without my consent*). They all blamed me for it, and they told *everyone*, that I was the whore. I am not a virgin, but I was also the whore! It didn't seem fair, because I knew that they wanted something out of me ... I think they wanted to see my diary. The diary, filled with all my thoughts, a memoir of my immigrant experiences. They wanted to see me dead, and wanted to be famous, because of my diary – my only refuge. Until I met God, of course, but what should I do, now? I am a rape victim, PTSD bound, and I am not a respectable _______, I was once before.

Would I have to keep on fighting these crazy thoughts? Men will never respect me, of my being, my wholesome personality or attitude. I am no longer a good person; instead, I am envisioned, as a whore once raped, now trying to make something out of myself. I am sad and depressed, but thank the Lord, that Effexor and Seroquel, are working overtime. ER meds, with its 100 and 200 mg, of itself, entwined, in my hyper-cerebellum. I feel so bad, ... I was raped, and everyone blamed me for it. They said, you can't prove it, you shouldn't have slept with your ex-boyfriends. Now...I am seen as a whore, prostitute, but quietly working behind Public Health. The

Whore-ristic Epidemiologist, the prize of the immigrant experience! Education, and PTSD, of how once a girl, gone insane. I don't feel that I will have hope of a bright, un-affected future. People will always see that side of me …the survivor side, and they will wonder, "how many people did she sleep with? And how MUCH baggage, does she have?"

I am no longer attractive, I am no longer a future mom, and I am no longer a future wife. Too many partners, and too many medications, to go through me. What would become of me? Where is my one, true, self (the happy one, the sweet one, the innocent one, the better person)?

What would happen now?

Black Berry

By Diana Kurniawan

Clone, clone, clone, batter my bone,
with anonymity, and pepper of reality.
I think I am made up, like a paprika,
mustard, tomato, evergreen lettuce in salads.

Grown, grown, grown, in a laboratory,
to scatter away the mysteries of birth.
One leg first, then two afterwards,
but who knew, the test came with none.

Abort, abort, abort, the results of birth,
almost like magazines, unsubscribe the egg.
With nameless authors, and stolen phrases,
the real egg, starts to disappear like dew.

Later, later, later, triplets are common,
and mothers will be scarce like melons.
You only find them in certain flu seasons,
but cancer will be here, STD's controlled?

Why, why, why, you making more of me?
Is one already too little, or one too many?
Stem of your research, was in good aim,
I hope your results, can do the same.

Confessions to a Dog

By Diana Kurniawan

Freddy (seat 1,3,4):
I know you hate me, and would like to see me dead, but here is a hint:

Hint #1:
People cheat on the turns in outrigger. There are fights ... don't participate.
Women get raped... especially innocent/inexperienced/battered ones.... don't get involved with one, until you know them well.
There are rich people in show business in outrigger, be careful of what you say. I didn't and got raped. He told me, he was Margaret Cho's relative, to keep my mouth shut; and I got flashbacks, because of his violence. Don't go to the parties in outrigger.... you'll get harassed in California, because you'll fight for the medal. Catalina is fun. People will make rumors out of you, so don't do anything stupid. Tell Radley, I said sorry. There are already some girls who've heard of you, in some outrigger teams.
They want to marry you, and they're beautiful; but you have some good ones back home.

You've hurt a good person.
Tell everyone I'm a rape victim, and you already know how bad.

You need to get that MBA. Go to LMU (Loyola Marymount University or UCLA) - get an MBA there. An enemy of mine went there, and got an MBA. I bet you'll end up with people from USC.
Don't drink.
AA is not for everyone.
Stop.
Get a life (like winning a medal or two in Outrigger).
If you've been acting, then be a good actor; otherwise, do some movie reviews.
Don't you dare stalk me...I know how to get, and do a "stay away order" now.
Good-bye Freddy.

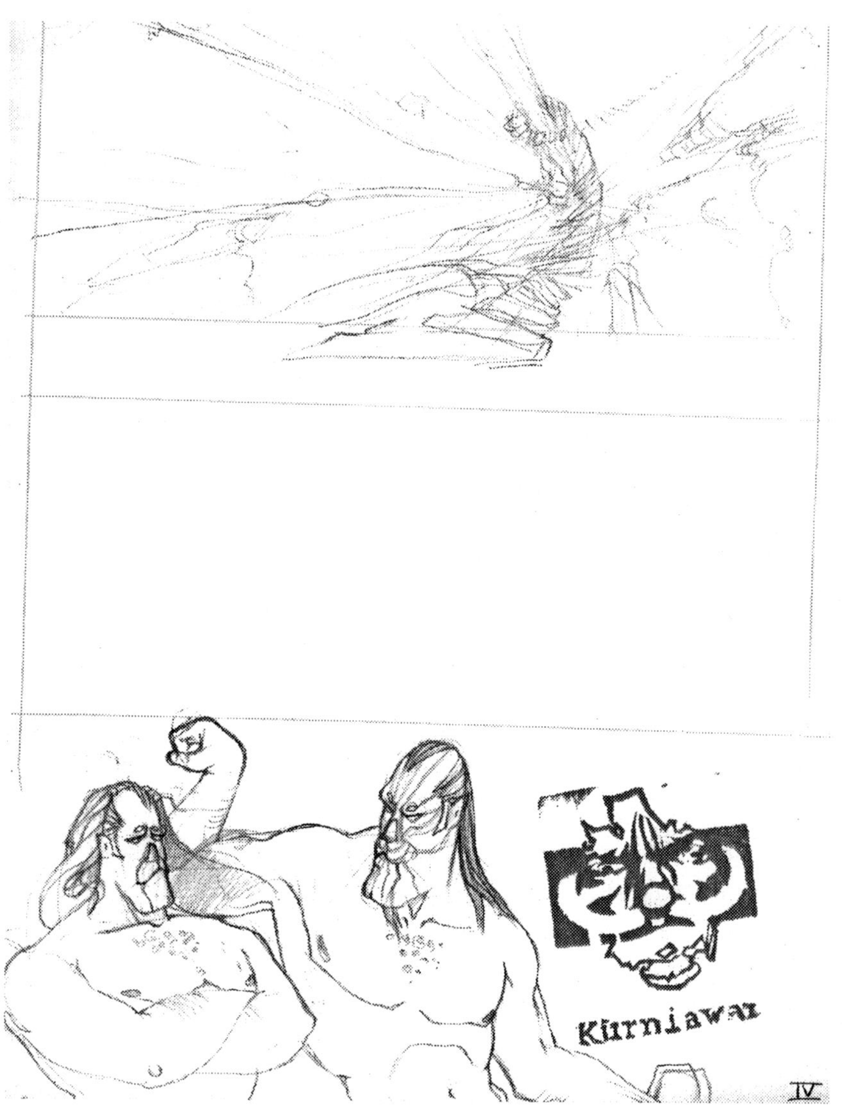

Beasts who kill for sex

The Rape You've Never Heard About!

Fiction by Diana Kurniawan

Good Person #8:

So they ***BOTH*** raped you?? The Crowfeathers???

Julee:

I don't know, I slept with one of the two brothers, but one night, he did not seem or *feel* like himself. I felt he was not the person I knew, and his face had slightly changed???

Good Person #8:

Did you meet the right person? Was the guy you asked to dinner, the same person you wanted to meet? Did you know both of them???

Julee:

I just know. I asked the younger of the Crowfeathers brothers, but I did not know them well.

Good Person #8:

You shouldn't have slept with either of them. Do you know, that sex before marriage, is just depression waiting to happen?

Julee:

I know, but I didn't know, he would be this abusive to me. I didn't know, they were both planning to rape me that way. I know they look like twins. I didn't know they planned to use me for sex. I didn't know, they would sneak a rape into my life, in the bedroom, to play around with my sexuality.

Good Person #8:

This is a tough call, because you didn't know them well. You were spiraling after your first relationship!

Julee:

I was raped by the first boyfriend I went out with. It was oral sex rape, but that is still rape, right??? (crying).

Good Person #8:

Yes! Oral sex is oral sex, but oral sex rape, is RAPE!!!!

Julee:

He told me, he wanted to try something new. I told him, I was ready to loose my virginity, but I didn't think he would have raped me.

Good Person #8:

Did you ever say *things*, that may lead him into thinking that you liked oral sex, or wanted him to treat you that way????

Julee:

He asked me if I liked "rough sex," but with my future husband, not now.

Good Person #8:

That's a VERY DANGEROUS STATEMENT!!! DO NOT SAY THAT TO ANYONE!!!! Because even husbands, could rape their wives!! It is called *spousal abuse*.

Julee:

Do you think that statement led to the rape?? I was in a mutually heavy "*petting*" relationship. We've never had sex, oral sex, anal sex, rough sex, ... until he just threw me on my roommate couch, to be victimized, by all means, oral sex.

Good Person #8:

Any type of rape is rape, sweetie. Whether it is oral rape, sexually abusive rape, anal sex rape, gang rape ... etc. Those are ALL RAPES!!!! Punishable by <u>imprisonment, or even the death penalty!!!</u>

Julee:

Do you think my first boyfriend, knew the Crowfeathers? I am so scared, they would retaliate, and murder me.

Good Person #8:

Stay clear from danger!! They have abused you, and yes, I am sure the Crowfeathers knew your first boyfriend. You met them in University, correct???

Julee:

They will spread my trauma to others???!!! They will make gossip, to kill me!! (sobbing, crying, flustered...)

Good Person #8:

If they knew each other, and *both* Crowfeathers have sneaked a sexual rape into your life, then yes, they have told others.

<u>You need to keep your grounds now.</u> Start living your perspective clearly, and be very careful, when you meet men!!

Julee:

Do you think men are sexual predators? I am scared, I do not want to be treated as a prostitute, the way the Crowfeathers have done to me.

Good Person #8:

Be careful when you go home, <u>at work</u>, and when you meet others, *especially* when you meet others!!

Some people choose to capitalize, on other people's sorrows, life, misfortunes, and personal lives. That's the basis of adultery, and crimes of passions.

<u>This world is filled with baggage, and we all have some.</u> Some people are in the business of burdening others, but there are honest people, who are in the business of saving lives.

<u>Remember your foundation, that morale will help in life.</u> This baggage is not really yours, give that baggage unto the law. You should report this, especially if they really have traumatized *your life.* God sees all things, and knows all things, and He could help. Seek, and ye shall find, …this time, your life will be anew.

Julee:

What should I do now? All have banished me, from *my* own life!! I am so sad and hurt, I can't describe my pain anymore … (sobbing). I have been victimized, and I know there are people out there, trying to send me a divorce; more trauma, more hate, more trash. They all wanted to trash my life … (sobbing), and please tell me it is not God!!!

Good Person #8:

Notice how these people, have a huge advantage compared to you. They feel they are righteous, and innocent. Trust me, there are times, when I feel JESUS=SATAN, BUT <u>SATAN IS NOT JESUS!!!!</u>

What you've experienced is man-made, and man, can be Satanic!!! Jesus is more powerful than this world, and *the one that is in you*, is *greater,* than the one who is in this world, 1 John 4:4.

People who have hurt you, this *much*, *and this far*, … <u>pray to satan</u>, <u>NOT JESUS, and DEFINITELY NOT **GOD!**</u>

Julee:

They've stolen personal things from me!! They've always kept a vengeance against me, and *now,* they've stolen my life, and ruined my future to pieces.

They've spread so much rumors against me! They've raped me, inside/out!! (sobbing, crying….)

Good Person #8:

What did they take??

Julee:

My personal diary (sobbing, curling her body from sorrows).

Good Person #8:

(Trying to keep Julee from falling to the ground)

Hear me!! Just breathe for 5 seconds, please, sweets!! ***Breathe, for 5 seconds!!!!!*** That's Not Much!!!! Here, (shoulders her arms, and walking to a more peaceful room), you can sit down.

You can pass this! It's behind a **door** that says, ***"I AM NOT ALONE!"*** **The same room as many victims have been!! I was there, don't give up!!**

Those brothers, rapists, evil men, hurtful boyfriends, who sought your death, filled their lives with crimes!!! YOU DID NOT!!!!

Julee:

HELP!!!!

Good Person #8:

We are in the business of saving lives!!! You can count on this person, to be sweet, humble, and kind. **KEEP ME WITH YOU!!!!** DON'T GIVE UP ON ME!!!! I AM A GOOD PERSON!!!!!

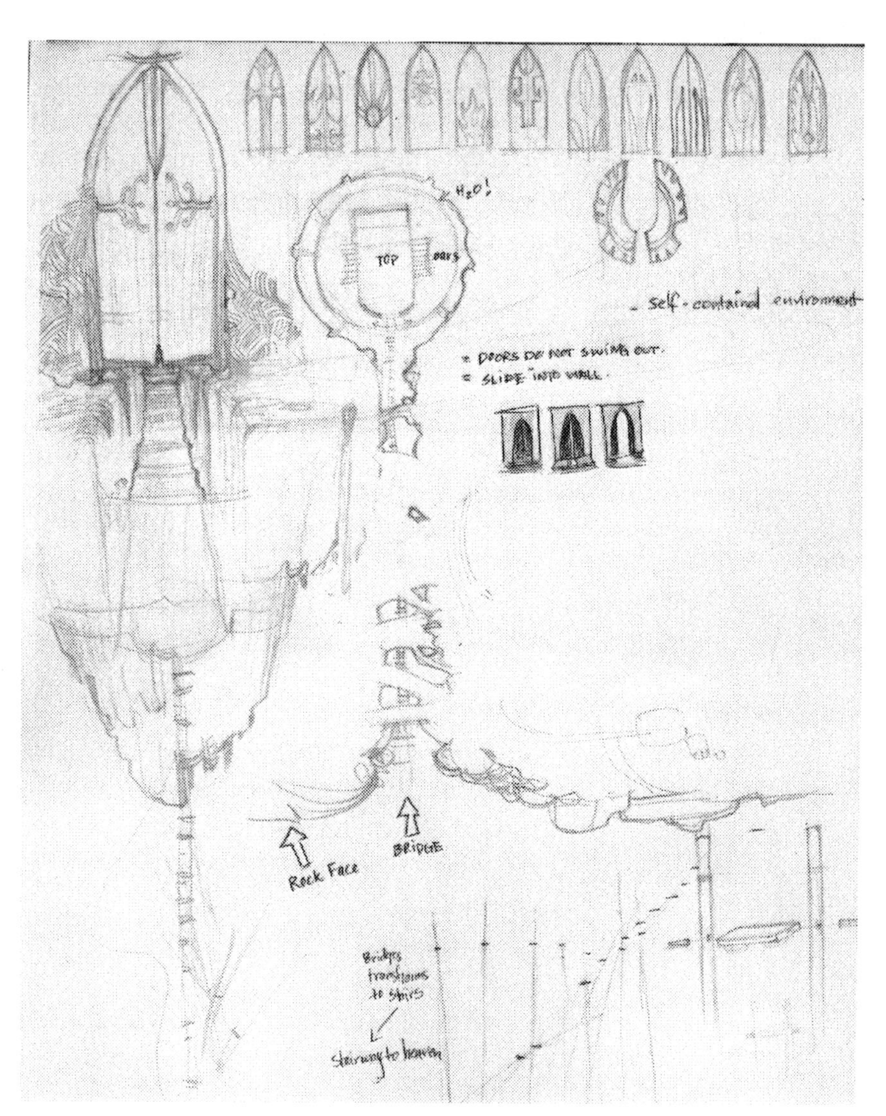

Heaven's door

Julee:

What if no one trusts me? There are so many people, who are against me!!!! (hurt, maybe suicidal, still sobbing …)

Good Person #8:

No one can trust anyone these days, but you can always trust yourself!! Especially, if God is with you, then you will succeed with God. <u>Try your best with your future.</u> <u>You have been given the right to live, the right, to be the best person you are.</u>

Julee:

I AM A GOOD PERSON!!!!

Good Person #8:

YES, YOU ARE!!!!! Try your best with this life, you are going to move one step at a time!!!

Julee:

One step at a time??? What if there are too many steps for me to step????

Good Person #8:

Then you need to call on the Lord, and pray with the steps that you have been given. Opportunities, don't come to everyone; but, if it comes, remember me, you are not alone with your life.

Julee:

I AM A GOOD PERSON!!!

Good Person #8:

YES, YOU ARE!!!

God and Politics are in the Eye of the Beholder

By Diana Kurniawan

What do you say to a rapist?
Do you say be careful to me, who's hurt?
Or do you say be careful to him, who broke the law?
I didn't think I was raped, like any other date rape.
So I don't know which one I should express.
Faith, or pain? Love, or anger? Immorality, or virtue?
I was never a good girl, always in trouble, hurt from the past, but do I really deserve this?
I had PTSD* due to rape, is that enough proof?
Is that enough to say?
Or need I go back in time, not shower, and cut off his penis, just to prove a crime?

I need to develop me, but then again, there is pain in me.
Just like poetry, I speak of pain, hidden in words.
So I go on with my life, and wonder if there is a god.

God of what? God of victims, who heals? Or god of crimes? Or God of politics, who decided that you are proven innocent, unless guilty. How can you be guilty, if you're innocent, and how can you be innocent, when there is PTSD? Isn't a crime, to misuse your power?

Sometimes it's hard to accept a crime; it's hard to accept, when there is no proof.

But still, isn't a crime to not do anything, when the proof, is in a hundred years of research, from Harvard, Yale, or anyone, who researched that mental illness due to rape, is evidence itself, of a crime? But then again, isn't a crime to wrongly accuse someone?

It's hard, it's really hard, because I don't know who's right.

The rapist, or the Law? God, or politics? Sometimes you can't ask for reasons. All I know is, that I've been healed, and I heard Him say,

Come baby, come to me,
come, and I will make you see.
That my kingdom is with Me,
and that's for being lonely

Come baby, don't go away,
come baby, please stay.
I'm the healer, and the redeemer too,
and that's for being lonely.

Oh baby, just stay in Me,
Oh baby, just stay in Me.
Then I will make you see,
loneliness with Me, is lovely.

Don't be afraid, don't give a care.
Don't lead astray, and loose me where,
you can't find me, and lost again,
and that's for being lonely.

Come baby, come to Me,
come, and I will make you see.
That my kingdom is with Me,
and that's for being lonely.

Then politics said, "It's YOUR FAULT!! <u>YOU TOOK A SHOWER</u>!!"

Where did the freakin' shower come from?

So politics said, "Ye shall overcome, Ye shall overcome …"

So maybe I should've reported earlier, but he tricked me ... he said he was a FRIEND, he said, he liked me. He never said, he *loved* me, but I, was in love with him.

I don't know, maybe I'm the slut, the whore, the prostitute, shiksa, or what ever Merriam-Webster said, a slut is supposed to be. But do sluts really deserve a rape? That's what every date rapist should know, and every rape victim should question. So report, <u>GOD DAMNED IT!!</u> Because it is never too late, and before it's too late, because God and the Law, are on your sides.

****Post-traumatic Stress Disorder, or PTSD***, is a psychiatric disorder that can occur following the experience, or witnessing of life-threatening events, such as <u>military combat, natural disasters, terrorists incidents, serious accidents, or violent personal assaults like rape</u>.
(National Center for PTSD – Online Definition).

Detective will ask questions

I'm Green and I'm Pretty

Fiction by Diana Kurniawan

Good Person #6:

<u>They stole your diary??</u>

Joia:

Yes, now I've been going to therapy, because the same people who stole my diary, stalked me; and gave me paranoia, and severe depression … (pain and frustration, written by her body language)

Good Person #6:

Were you diagnosed with these things? These conditions?

Joia:

Yes, not paranoia, but severe depression (starting to cry).

Good Person #6:

Do you have proof, that your diary was stolen?

Joia:

Yes, random people at school would say, and yell, words .. that I've written in my personal diary. Although, some were written in a foreign language, they would say those exact words, and psychologically abuse me. They would say something mean, … something I had written the night before.

Good Person #6:

Wow, were these "frat" (F&C*ing Brats) boys, and sororities chicks, the people who stole your diary?

Joia:

Yes, they would carry pieces of paper, with photo-copied versions, of my personal diary.

Good Person #6:

This is a very racist, and dangerous situation. I've known many girls who committed suicide, because of "hazing" or crimes, involving the "Greek" system.

Joia:

I was not associated with them!! I did not do anything to these people … Why did they hate me so much?!?!?! (sobbing, crying in pain).

Good Person #6:

The "Greek" System has a caveat, called "hazing." It's a terrible, travesty, tragedy, considering how young they are, when they did this. They sometimes rape innocent women, to prove they are of higher status. I wish I could stop these hazing tactics!!!!

Joia:

The "Greek" frats and sororities at my school, stole my personal diary, because I knew a rape victim. That was the reason why they hated me, because they felt I was a piece of trash, for remembering the tragedy. They felt that they wanted to be "GOD," and toy my life apart. To make sure, that I will loose every step of life, until I commit suicide.

Good Person #6:

So they "hazed" you, because you've seen a crime?? Or knew of a crime?

Joia:

They wanted to write about it, and I was not willing to play their game.

Good Person #6:

The "Greek" System, do this all the time!!! They have raped women, commit hate crimes, abused immigrants, and sometimes murder. Were you a sorority pledge? Which sororities did this? We can take a police report.

Joia:

I was not involved in any "Greek" sororities, and I was just another girl at school. I was a victim, because some of the girls, classmates, and others, were jealous of my diary, so they stole it. They copied it, to be sold to people, for money.

Good Person #6:

You told people about the diary?

Joia:

Yes, because I had told someone of the rape I knew of. They became jealous, because they felt I was a criminal, for not reporting.

Good Person #6:

Why did you do that??? Why did you tell people about your diary???

Joia:

I didn't think people would try to hurt me, with my own diary!! I thought they would stay away from me!!

Good Person #6:

It was a crime waiting to happen, you know that??? Did you report to the authorities, about the friend who got raped? At least?

Joia:

No, I didn't tell anyone, but some people I trusted. I was wrong, I admit it, but I tried to encourage the rape victim to report herself. I was a green-card holder (permanent resident), and I was scared, that I will not have a citizenship, because I saw a crime, or even heard of one.

Good Person #6:

Did the victim have a citizenship?

Joia:

No, she was illegal, she only had a temporary visa.

Good Person#6:

This tragedy is not your fault, because I bet the rapist had a citizenship. Was the rapist a "FRAT" boy??? They usually act like they belong in a 1950s Confederacy barracks sometimes!!! But there are criminals, with citizenships, and it is NOT your fault.

Joia:

What should I do now? Now that I am a victim of theft, and my personal diary is stolen from me???? (scared, still crying ...)

Good Person #6:

There is nothing you can do, sweets. Keep quiet for a while, and try not to think about how these people, hurt you.

These criminals, did it for their personal glory. Frat boys, and sorority chicks are the same; they do this often, and you did the right thing.

Joia:

Should I have reported about my friend's rape? I was only 16, and I was a green-card holder. I didn't know that much about hazing, and crimes like these.

Good Person #6:

You were trying to protect yourself from this crime, so what happened with her was a crime. You did the right thing, in trying to help her to report the rape. Rape victims should always report immediately.

Joia:

I was traumatized because of what happened. I was worried for my family, and I felt that I was placed, in a no way out situation. I felt framed, and I didn't know what to do, to help a rape victim. I don't think anyone could immediately respond, at 911.

Good Person#6:

What you have just said, is the basis of why the "Greek" frats and sororities, stole your diary. Remember, if you go to court with this tragedy, the people who hurt you were wrong.
I do not want you to be a victim, because of *their* crimes.

This is not like a fictional event, this is *real* life. You were right, in trying to protect yourself, and your family; especially when it comes to rape, and attempted murder.

Those types of crimes are not at the same level as shoplifting, or petty theft; these types of crimes, are about blood.

Joia:

I am scared for my life, because I have a little brother; and I want him to succeed in life. I felt that I have been robbed, at my chance in life, because the rape victim wanted me to report, about the crime she experienced. I did not know what to do, at 16 years old, especially when it was about a crime like this.

Good Person #6:

Did you advice your friend to get counseling? It's never too late for any rape victim to start a new life.

Joia:

I told her to stay at the church she goes to, but I left to university. I just didn't know people whom I told about this, in university, would try to kill me, or steal my diary.

I am scared for my future, and now, of people who've stolen my properties. I was trying to protect my little brother, and my parents.

Good Person #6:

I agree in protecting your brother, and parents. I am proud of you, but you shouldn't have told friends, friends can be enemies too....we all know.

Joia:

(crying...) Do you think I will have a good life? Do you think I will have a good future??

Good Person #6:

You will have to forgive a lot more people than you think. That's what happens to victims, we need to forgive, since that's what we can only do sometimes.

Joia:

I feel cheated. I feel that the rape victim, and the rapist, have raped me, especially at 16 years old. This situation hurts me, more than her. I feel my family, will be blamed for something I did not do. I feel framed, and victimized, by the rape victim.

Good Person #6:

I would feel the same way, but you've helped her. You have helped her, in encouraging her to report, and suggesting her of a decision to follow the church.

I believe in God too, I will pray for all of you, and there is nothing wrong with loving your family, make sure you are well taken care of.

All in a Day's Work with Financial Crisis

By Diana Kurniawan

"What?" I asked.

"No, I thought I'd switch subjects between your hair, and my daughter not having a pet," Daisy said.

"I'm hurt," I hear an insult. "No, I'm not trying to hurt you, she likes your hair, because you're like Barbie," she commented.

"I think dogs have nothing to do with hair," I noticed deceit. "I'm saying my daughter loves your hair, because she doesn't have dogs. I just want to treat you like a sister, a friend," the 40 year old Financial Advisor said. I just thought, 27 year olds shouldn't be treated this way. Then, to have a financial advisor, tell *you* how much your hair, resembles a dog's hair, IS UNCALLED FOR!!!

Immigrant Lover

Fiction by Diana Kurniawan

Rape is not accepted among women, at least in the Asian American community, and now, at the level of all Americans. Did we start with a bad seed? Is this why there is so much pressure? Or is it because we have a lot of technology, and commercial garbage of violence, and bad drama about pressure, or how to *NOT* handle it well? We started to laugh at other people's dilemmas, and we feel better, about how people are suffering. "Oh, she committed herself to psychotherapy??? I knew it!!! I am so dead on!!" said a church member. "There are too many people like her," said another. "But it's her fault! She never came out of it! She knew she had to work triple the amount of time, compared to born natives of United States!!"

"Its not her fault, her education was a misfortune, she didn't really learn very well. She worked a lot, and that's all she knew how to do. She didn't really learn a lot of culture, and knowledge, that's how most of them are …future Asian porn stars," a militant Arian would say. Our pastor said, “I’m sorry, but no one deserves bad karma.” I stood there, feeling a bit worried, because I, was also in the position of them. I do what other people do….the normal stuff.

I was also a kid with a lot of talent, a lot of charisma….seeking attention, and a lot of issues to deal with, at home, and at school. I was the typical kid, who would sit in the back corner of the class room, and sleep. The one who would sit in the middle, and talk to other students, about the latest gossip at school, who is doing what…and how I didn’t have a boyfriend. I was similar to some kids at school…self absorbed. We worry about what will happen to us, after high school, who will help? Then, what happens if we don’t have money for college? Because, in East Los Angeles, there are a lot of gang-bangers, rapists, alcoholic murderers, and law violators, that even high school students, can become one.

There has to be a way for me to deal with this, and get ahead to the big schools, right? There is a way to succeed, and we know it’s called …work. Then, what about language barriers? Am I still considered a minority? Now that Asian Americans, are everywhere? Do they care if I had to take English as a Second Language course, or does that make things even worse?

“Do you know the trouble my parents had to go through?” is what I think, when asked, if I would ever go back to my mother country, and stay there. “You don’t seem to like it here little girl…do you miss home? Why don‘t you go home or visit?” often is the question. “But there is violence, sir,” I said. That was a sample of one-minute conversation, at a teen club, in the ghetto. I went, because I didn’t know who to turn to, and who to talk to, about social pressures of an immigrant from a violent country. Could I work with you?

Talk about competition in school of who's cleaner? How girls treated you, because you're pretty, or because you have talent, or rich, or maybe because you're the type who can kill to get to the top. Violence, is now a part of the immigrant experience. It has become a necessary roughness category, for people who are jealous. Hurt them, so they can't talk, and if they do… they will never find a job. Talk about movie stars getting raped, and girls on the verge of fame, getting hurt; then they can see for themselves, who really deserves to find the original voice. The one with REAL stories to tell, because if you haven't come close to being shot by a rap star, or physically involved with a hip-hop cornerstone (called teen pregnancy); then you may not be deserving of success. You haven't been killed! So you can't be successful!! If you're an immigrant, you need to ask permission. Permission from the serial killers, funded by the biggest mafias in the world …urban terrorists.

Then, you can see the difference, between the strong, and the weak. The weak, they have a ring, … a ring of violence, surrounded by past enemies. The types of enemies, with more money than you! The whole cyclic position, of how poverty, can never be balanced or broken, is not a rumor anymore, it is the norm.

Do you love immigrants??

Comfort Foods

By Diana Kurniawan

Whether we like our situation(s) or not, we could tell by the way we cook. When angry or sad, uncomfortable, and awry, we can see how we peel that potato, or think of the signs we show; because we love to taste that warm soup, made of rice. Love could muster inside that bowl of porridge, with green onions, and fried scallions, with perhaps slices of chicken, to flavor the low-fat diet (optional). Pell the potato away, along with your garbage of hate, injustice, or feelings of restlessness; blink, and take a seat to relax. Breathe, smile, and think funny foods.

Let's cook for comfort.

You should always start with some clean hands. Wash it up, rub your fingers in every possible way, while wondering why liquid looks like water. There are even bubbles involved! Put some soap on your hands, to make sure no minute living creatures, are in the crevices of your palms. Don't be afraid to lather it on! It's okay, that hard day is about to be over, because the bubbles look tiny, and your eyes are still working.

Let's talk porridge.

Now that your hands are clean, place a little napkin on your lap, because you are sitting on that dining chair, after a hard day, and wondering why it was this way. Then look at the napkin, on your lap. See how it is flat, clean, comfortable, and it's yours! Enjoy that little piece of napkin; then laugh a little, wrinkle your face to show you're happy. It's cool that way.

Now get 3 cups of rice, and place it in a pot.

Don't forget to think of the little creatures in your palms again, because it might live in your rice too! Again, wash the rice inside the pot, with warm water this time; and fill the pot, until the water reaches one inch, above rice level. Use both hands, sink your hands in the pot, and make the rice run around your hands, inside the water. How strange it is to be cleaned by you? The one with some problems, and perhaps emotional trauma, but now YOU ARE COMFORTABLE.

After washing the rice three times, you could turn on the stove, to medium heat, and cook the rice. Put a gallon of water, or just half way from the top, of the pot, to make sure you have enough water, to turn the rice into soup.

Don't forget to dry the bottom of the pot, and remember that when water meets fire, you will hear crackling noises; and you will get scared. Now, stir the rice in a pot, for an hour or so, and you are not allowed to leave the cooking station until it is done. You should always take care of your dish, before it blows up. Personally, individuals in today's society would multi-task, and cut some green onions, in thin radial slices, to use as decoration for the juicy food you are about to have.

By this time, you are probably tired, and would like to go to sleep.

If the rice dish is not done, put a teaspoon full of salt, with three dashes of pepper, for flavor. Then, turn off the stove, cover the pot, and put it inside the refrigerator (*again*, to stop bacterias from coming into your foods.). Please do the same, to the green onions, and cover the container they are in, with saran wrap. When you are ready to take sometime to relax, just go to the bedroom, and snore.

When you wake up, after that 30 minutes nap of yours, go back to the kitchen, and finish cooking the porridge. This time, until the rice is soft, and "JEWY" (juicy and gewy), almost like Elmer's glue consistency. Sprinkle some green onions, and a squirt of soy sauce, to finish the dish. Unless, you dash some pepper, then your porridge will be spicy. Finally, enjoy the warm taste of your delicious porridge (after your nap) and thank God you're comfortable!

Breakfast at Tiffany's Shack

Fiction by Diana Kurniawan

I am a girl, who turned out to be a magnet. Then, stabbed as a sacrifice, to be fed to the dogs, to satisfy their hunger, until no more satiation exist. I was left slashed, open in pieces. My name is Tiffany, and I was set up for a crime. Who would know, that she is hurt, in pain and heaving, from abuse by others? Do you think it is possible, for anyone to be given this treatment? She is an immigrant. She is poor, economically disadvantaged, and she will never amount to anything, but she is pretty. Who knows?? Perhaps, one day she will do porn, maybe perform at strip joints?? What do you think? The clatters in my brain, comes out to play, and sometimes it says, "yeah right. That's really going to happen." Then the insides of my body, uncontrollably reached the telephone, dialed for 911, "Crisis Emergency Center, Santa Monica..." the police dispatcher said.

I said to myself, "I was raped!!!! What should I do, mister???!!!! Please help me!!!!" The phone police dispatcher said, "what is going on? Are you okay? Is everything all right? Where are you? Do you need an ambulance?"

"I was raped by a surfer sir!!! What should I do? His name is Satanic Cho! What should I do?" I said clamoring, yet understandable. "We will send a police! We can take a statement, and we can take you to the hospital," said the lady. This was Culver City, nothing should happen in Culver City, but a rapist is there. What should I do? He lives in the same town, same name, different identity, but criminal record.

I said to myself, "Tiffany, it's real. I was raped ... it's not your fault! It's okay, you are going to be okay."

Then she called a friend, "Diana, please tell me what I should do? I want to report. What should I do? I need your help. I think you understand." She said, "Don't play the victim here! - Don't think that you are a rape victim! - You were at that barbeque party drinking!! - You placed yourself in that situation!! - I don't believe you! - Plus, with your record, I don't think that there is a possible way, that you were raped."

She said, all in one sentence.

"But I am not playing a victim, I AM A VICTIM! Diana, please believe me, I am not lying." I said, with an almost crying tone, confused, and feel disgusted. "I don't believe you, I know you were sleeping around! I don't think that could happen! I think it's rough sex." I was baffled. I was not sure if she was a friend anymore. I had relationships, and I was not sleeping around. "If you are doing this for the money, it's not worth it Tiffany!" she said. "What money?? Is Cho rich, or something?" I was scared, of his retaliation. I have heard of surfers' parties, and girls getting raped, and I was not supposed to be her. This time, I was the dumb victim. The one, who didn't anticipate him to be a rapist; although, he was talking about rape, *before* I was raped.

"What do you think we should do? If we were to rape someone, Tiffany?" he would ask, "you know, so she won't *think* she was raped?"

"Ask her out the next day, so she would think that it was a mutual thing, or things got really ugly, and heavy burdened. Just say that she was just really hot that night, and she wanted to do it too, but *unsure*; so *you* just took the initiative," I said jokingly. It did happen to me.

"God, what should I do now?? JESUS, PLEASE HELP!!!!!!" I would cry, and then I ran to the door, and walked outside, screaming, "SOMEONE DID VOODOO ON ME!!!!!! PLEASE HELP ME!!!!!! HE RAPED ME!!!!!!!!!! What should I do??"

I contemplated suicide. I was not supposed to be in this position. I was not supposed to be hurt. WHAT SHOULD I DO NOW?!!!!!!!?!?!?!?!?!?!

Girls go to surfing parties all the time, and yes, they had booze there, drinks, eats, grubs, and he had pot, grass, and who knows what else. I was not supposed to find out, but I did, and I was raped because of it.

He had a knife, and he was angry. I was not understanding the situation, because he was angry at me, and I didn't know why. "You f*Cked up my sister's name!!!" I was not sure, why he had brought his sister into the situation. He must have been a big person, somewhere?? Or he was lying. I was not sure, why he was doing anything?!?!! Rough sex is in ... an inexperienced women don't know, especially virginal queens, or immigrant women. This is the 'in' thing, and the 'in-crowds' know the victims, to be perpetrated against. This is the warning signs, he will rape, then he will ask you out; and claim rough sex. Remember that people, and remember the innocent immigrant women too! This is the deal girls, friends, lovers, they know what they want, and they will have it. The crime is already positioned, into the places most wanted. In turn, you are in the picture, framed; even if you want to get out. You could try for the rest of your life, because he will make sure your life, *depends* on him. But really, it starts with you.

"If you retaliate, I will bomb your house!!!! I WILL BOMB YOUR WHOLE FAMILY!!!!!" He said, with a knife in his left hand, facing me, as I left his house the next morning, after a whole night of "rough sex."

I was not sure what happened, rough sex, or forced copulation. Either way, nothing should have been roughed up, especially not my vagina, chastity, mentality, morality, health, and my personality. This is the perceivable danger, *nothing happened*, she was asking for it. IS that RIGHT??? Tiffany wore green t-shirts, cargo pants, with lots of pockets on the side….she was not even a lesbian, that everyone thinks. No, she did not dress ‘girlie,’ because she was a tomboy, and she was honest, and innocent. She did not have proper sex education, just as many others had. How could you teach someone, without experience? And how could you teach someone, who is not meant to do it before marriage? The bottom line was, rape is rape, and she was raped; whether she was experienced or not. IT IS WRONG, especially for the future. She was raped, and not a single soul could take that ‘experience,’ away from her; not even the devil, since he wanted it to stay. You can lie about it, and it peaks at the most pinnacle of crimes, called fabrication of evidence. Rapists know the deal, they just got smarter now, so you may need to write some penal codes down!!

Does this happen to surfer girls? Women? Ladies? Sluts? Whores? Fornicators? Yes, one out of three women were raped, and that is in America alone; now we can talk about Thailand. Just kidding.

It's Not Just the Rain in Seattle!!!!

Fiction by Diana Kurniawan.

Suicide my a*s!
I'm pis#ed off, that I think of it!
But I forgot, that it's not the trend,
or is it? For someone who's depressed,
and pissed off at the world, that
nothing ever goes right, because,
I'm a stupid suicidal a*s.
Whose time seems like imprisonment,
tied, with mind boggling reactions.
Almost chemical, like sex on the beach,
with too much alcohol, and too little
time to run, and too many people chasing
along, your own grounds or sand.
Suicide my a*s!!
Try it, and it will kill your own a*se!
Suicide my a*s!!!
F*%k it I say, it is the worst thing
to do, when you're a suicidal ass!

Could You Understand My Troubles?

By Diana Kurniawan

DONOVAN SAID:

"Sometimes my conscience precedes me. Thoughts of negativity, and other disturbances in life, come into my brain, and asks me, "so, what shall you think about today? Is there a bizarre, twisted misfortune in your future?" Shall I stop that questioning thought, or shall I try to see what it really will guide me through? Is it true, that some worries are good, and some worries are bad?? How come my worries, are all bad?? Or actually, out of my control."

"I am a Christian, yet I have so little faith in my life. I try to find my solace through the Lord, and talk to Jesus, when times are low, and tides are high. Yet, I am always caught up in the moment, and get in more deep thoughts of depression."

"I seemed to be in a spiraled conundrum, chagrin conscience. Where should I go, and what medication should I take to stop this? I'm already seeing a psychotherapist, for my meds, and a counselor, to make myself peaceful, and calm. Why am I like this? There is a void in me…do others feel this way too?"

Good Person #1:

"A void is something to be filled, with something of worth; something substantial, that you can grasp, and put into motion. It is okay, everyone had bad thoughts, dreams, experiences. Why should you be any different?"

"If there is a time, when I can actually say to myself, I AM HEALTHY, I AM GREAT, and I AM HAPPY!!! That's the time when you can see, that there is a miracle in the moment of your life."

"Do you believe in miracles?"

DONOVAN SAID:

"I do, but how do you know, you are having a miraculous moment? Everyone tells me, they can feel God, but I have had so much pain in my life, that I am not sure God loves me."

Good Person #1:

"Well, … why wouldn't the Lord love you? We are all sinners anyway, why can't you except that of yourself, and let the Lord love you? Are you afraid of love, that it makes your life, hard to live?"

Hula Girl picks up her pieces

DONOVAN SAID:

"I am longing for love, but love never came. I am 45 years old, and yes, I am lonely. Who is left out there for me? I am already old, and I feel that life, had cheated me, out of my true potential. Do you believe in that? Do you believe, that even the good people in our world, don't become happy, instead, are wounded by those who don't deserve happiness?"

Good Person #1:

"Yes, life can be unfair, and bad people, are an example of that."

"I wish I could show you, I wish you could see my heart. It is harmed, but it healed. Just because you are alone, doesn't mean you are not loved. Please believe me, I am not going to give you a rose colored picture, for you to see. I am just like you, and Jesus was crucified, while he was single as well."

"I feel bad that you felt this way, because I know what it was like to be hurt, and to be beaten to the ground. We survive though, you are still alive, and as I."

DONOVAN SAID:

"You are telling me that I am lucky. I wish I could see it, but I have seen the homeless, the sick, the tortured, the diseased, the dying, the sinful natures of some. Could you understand my troubles? Please, tell me what you can say to people like these ..."

Good Person #1:

"I don't know what to say, but I know how to listen … that's why I pray. I pray a lot."

DONOVAN SAID:

"I'm on a prayer hunger season. I don't know what else to ask from Him. I don't know what else could go wrong."

Good Person #1:

"Neither do I, but I just pray. I don't know what else to show, or tell you. I do want you to feel better. I wish I am able to give you everything, that is good in life, but you must caulk the leakage, to avoid more danger of your coherent mind."

DONOVAN SAID:

"I can't do it. I don't want to live. I have no one else in life, well… perhaps my parents, ex-husbands, kids who don't show up at dinners in my house. I can't live like this."

Good Person #1:

"I can't watch you die in vain. It happens many times, please don't let it happen again. You are so strong, you've done well, you've got to show me, and your friends. You haven't told me what your next good move would be."

DONOVAN SAID:

“I have no one. Don’t you understand?”

“Nobody …”

Good Person #1:

“But … there is me.”

DONOVAN SAID:

“I can’t see you … you are not here, who are you?”

<u>Good Person #1:</u>

“How did you find me? Do you remember?”

DONOVAN SAID:

“Will you take care of me?”

Good Person #1:

“I wish I can do that all the time, but stand girlie …stand …it’s a part of being a person.

We can stand on our own two feet. I want you to do the same.”

DONOVAN SAID:

“I wish to die soon … God please take away my life.”

Good Person #1:

"This wish, is wishful emptiness. Emptiness, is just a cycle, like loneliness. Both feelings are something you can break, when you choose too. They are words, that implies a person's heart; a heart which can choose to love, as no one can compare."

DONOVAN SAID:

"I am tired of no love, more emptiness, and loneliness, I want to leave my space."

Good Person #1:

"Get closer to heaven, and be more down to earth. Wait for your turn, my dear …"

DONOVAN SAID:

"What's another day …

Good Person #1:

"Exactly … what's to it …might as well live it. Be good yeah?"

<u>DONOVAN SAID:</u>

"Yeah … thanks God."

Good Person #1:

"That's what angels are for ☺."

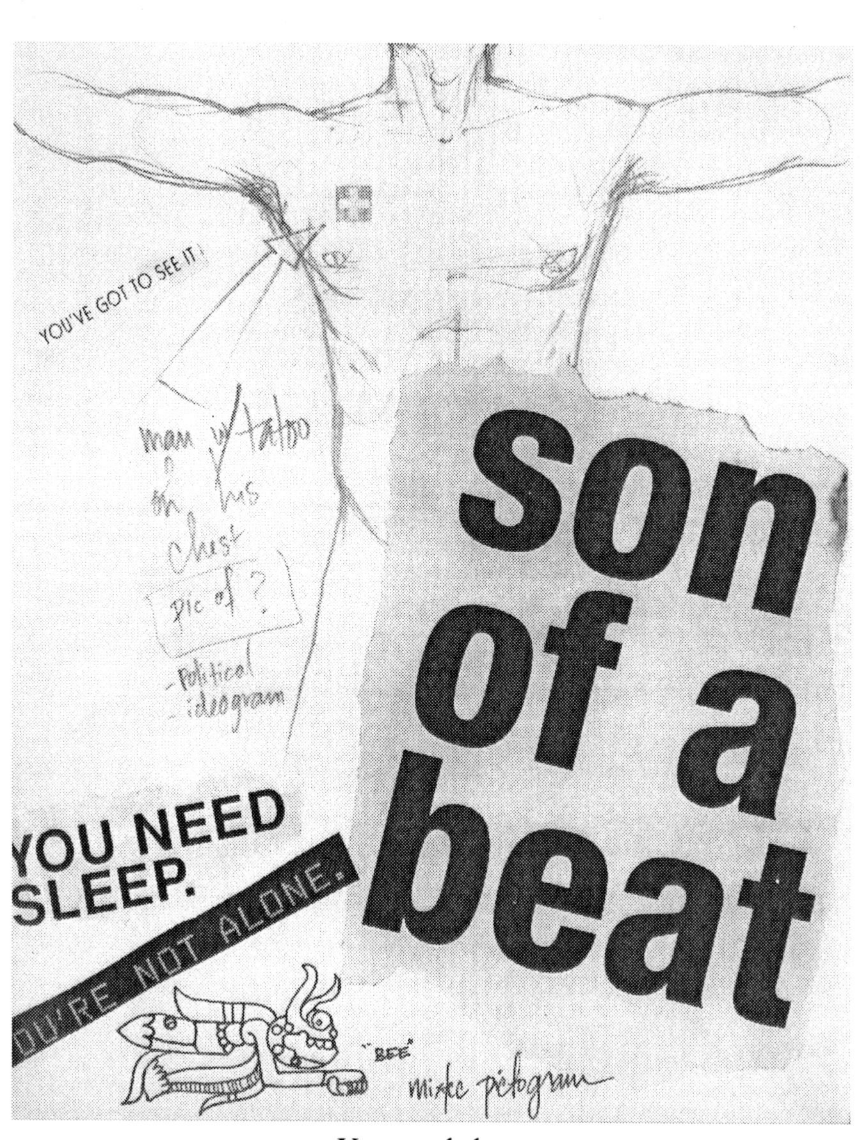

You need sleep

Jesus was Single

Fiction by Diana Kurniawan

As he gently laid his hands upon her head, the murmured, still, small voice, from within said, "I still love you. You are my wife." A common remark, after a year long affair, this pastor had with his brother's wife. "I have always loved you," she replied, as he started to cry, and walked his way into the long corridor, of civil court rooms.

Where should we draw the line? He's a Christian, and he's married, but wasn't that a sin? "She was not the girl of my dreams," the 50 years old man, said to his lawyer.

"May the one you love, be the one you marry," is what everyone kept telling newlyweds. It is difficult to stay with a person without loving them, let alone marrying them. Do we, as an individual, have to risk our desire, and dreams of that someone, for a lesser than expected man or woman, for a soul mate, because … of our own fears for divorce?

Let's take a situation where a pretty lad, and a beautiful young woman, intended to marry. "Pastor, she is the one," he said. "He is my one, true love," she said. "I bless you with everlasting love and happiness. I will join your hands in marriage." What a perfect relationship, on the surface. Then years passed (with some *evidential mishaps*), beyond their wildest dreams, … things take toll. She wanted the "real" man of her dream! She wished for the taller, rugged, Brendan Fraser look-alike, who is great in fixing the clogged toilet, and read Shakespeare to her, on Saturday mornings. He does exist, and yes, many women love him, but that is just the trouble … many women love him (even his wife). No, they are not ALL married, but when you are in your late 30s, or 40s, … chances are, they are ☹.

So, do we women, settle for less, and commit ourselves to a life with a geek, or a nerd, or an ugly guy????? Doesn't that sound harsh? Should we settle for less? Or should we, uphold our own desires, and be honest, to wait and marry. Okay let's slow down, should we, women, go-out with these lesser than wonderful male counter parts, and say to ourselves, "I'm being nice. If he asks me to marry him, that's fine. Who else is going to do it?" If you don't like the person, no chemistry, no sparks, no relationship. Don't get married until you are ready, with the right person. Believe.

The problem is, we are human, ready or not. That does not mean, we need to lessen our expectations, sleep around, or even date like a maniac; because we may be cheating ourselves, of our own pleasures in life, that is ordained by God, as ours. Be real people! Don't place yourselves, in these situations. That will one day, causes you to be haunted by sins, or lead you to a bitter world, and cause havoc on your future. It was all a bunch of small-scales mistakes, *we always seem to see it as such.*

Until one day, a pastor admitted to his sin, of years of affairs, with his closest friend, *his brother's wife.* Things don't, JUST HAPPEN??? Then we all see our situations, and we MUST be able to say, "That guy is a lying, cheating, bastard, no shame, and guilty, wolfish-son-of-the-devil!!!!"

We cannot say, "Infidelity, aahhh yes, that thing ... yes, it happens. Now what were we talking about just now? Brendan Fraser? Yeah … he's cute. I'd like to have an affair with him!!!" No!!! That's not right. RIGHT?!?!??!?!?!?!? At least, that's what the Bible told me so.

Don't be scared, families will always be there, at least good ones. Yours will come, therefore, get ready. Future husbands, and wives, need to be the "real person of your dreams." The truth will come out, even when you are not looking for it. That's why I believe in God.

YOU CAN DO IT!!!

By Diana Kurniawan

I noticed when he drinks his beverages, his pinky would remain straight, despite the others: thumb, forefingers, and even the ever-famous middle fingers, would be curved along the surface of the glass, of water he holds. I started to do the same, but when I was 14, I didn't even notice it before. My brother, who was turning 11, yelled in the middle of our dinner, "Hey PAPI!!! Your pinky goes out!!!" My father started to laugh, and he once again wondered, why children watch the silly actions, of those around them. Instead of listening to his stories, of Chairman Mao, or Guruh Soekarno. I supposed not all children, would listen and watch, instead asks questions. "How come plants know how to grow up from the soil, instead of inside the ground?"* I mean … a lot of plants do that!!" I asked my father, and he said, "that is why you need to read!!"

It's all about being a quick thinker. Children have a short attention span, please keep up.

When parents teach their children, they hope to be listened upon; at times, challenged by our inquiring minds. Maybe, just maybe, they would remember your teachings, more than the fight you had with the man at the gas station (because he was honking, one too many times). Children watched the reactions of adults, and from time to time, they would judge adults; because we forgot, "how to be a good person." It's not your fault, I am sure there are plenty adults who abuse children, molest them, and throw them inside the fiery furnace, like the wicked witch from Hansel and Gretel. Yet, do we want to turn into a criminal? Does the eye of the innocent change your situation, or your personality? Does parenting become a hassle, and cause marriages to break apart? Since, her (the wife's) views, and his (the husband's) views, are not complementary? How could you call yourselves bad parents, when you have a heart to raise good children? So your kids are not models, or sports icon, but hard work pays off. Don't be sad you're not a doctor, there are a bunch of politicians who had offsprings. Don't be sad you're not rich, Enrico Fermi was an immigrant, and he built the atomic bomb. I'm sorry you're divorced. I'm truly sorry.

In any case, kids are funny aren't they? They are the sole purpose, the world will continue to have joy, generations, and a future; but it all depends on how, we (adults), raise them since their birth. You know how the saying goes, "if you make a big mistake, your grand children will pay for it." If you grow up with the wrong lessons, the fruits will show up, when you turn into an adult. Then, you will need therapy, and hope that you will be healed in time, before you become a parent yourself (and ruin someone else's life).

Then, as I kept questioning myself, and what happened when I was a child? I know one thing, ... I can feel the love of my parents. They did not lie. When they are angry, they showed it. When they are proud of me, they hugged. They never paid me, to listen, or get good grades; because, we had enough troubles with paying the rent, than allowances. I saw them sweat, and cry. I saw them beaten, by the years, with struggles of finances, racism, immigration, sibling rivalries, and most of all, I saw their wrath. They were never shy, of showing how, what, or why, they felt a certain way. They shouted, and they shouted, but never failed to make us listen, by showing us how creative they are. They would tell us, "develop your gifts, if you don't have the resources, just do it anyway. You could find solace through it."

So does watching, prove to mean more than listening? Then why does the term, "the harsh things you hear, last longer than the positive remarks" exists? Where did we go wrong? Why did my child end up in gangs, raped a young teen, or became a high school, or college drop out? Which is it? Tell them, or show them? Nature, or nurture? Passive, or active? There are no right, or wrong answers in parenting. Parents don't need to spoil their children, to make sure they have a good future. Resources are for the lucky, so be creative people, and keep up!!

They remembered to put us, children, first; and reminded us, to watch a good movie once in a while, when we have the time and money. My dad would ask me to walk with him, because he kept getting lost when we arrived in United States. They told us, "sex is for marriage, otherwise, you will get depressed" and "be careful with friends, they can hurt you, more than strangers." They were real.

They didn't bother to give us Christmas presents, when there was no money. "We need the money to pay for rents kids, let's just go out to eat as a family, and drink tea." We, children, grew up faster, not necessarily good; but we did not grow on materials, we got stronger. I admit, I stole some things, and they hated me, because they didn't want me to go to jail. My parents worked, I remembered that most … they worked hard. Then one day, "Diana, we need you to help us with money, we don't have enough." I was sad, because I know my parents were going to ask me, many more times.

As I become older, more capable to earn money, I started to count, how many dollars I have spent helping my family. Then I realized, what it meant, to be "whole-hearted." I told them, "I need the money this month, Mom. I can't help you all the time!" I let them become sad, but I need the money, for myself. "You're so selfish, Diana!!! I will always help my parent, when I grow up," said my younger brother, whose 3 years advantage, made a difference, in understanding what a "burden" meant. I made sure, I was respected. I went to graduate school.

I stopped listening to them (my parents) in college, because they kept asking for help, and I wanted to, for once, be a kid. Then, they stopped asking, and I realized, I was a kid. I finally understood, the power of being a parent, where they need to live, make a living, and create a life for their offsprings. They were handed a situation, they took it, and hope to turn it into gold. "We need to struggle together, all of us, we are a family," my father told me, and I realized that the word "struggle" also involved: the rolling earthquakes, thunder, lightning, or the devil's hands, and disrespectful families, who gossiped about us being poor. I, understood. I knew my parent's plan … it all came in time.

"I am sure, the devil kept wanting us to fail," my father told us that, so we all believed in each other.

Now, we are not poor, we are satisfied. Most parents kept telling us, you are children, and they are parents, but my father said, "Our family is what it is, OUR family." There is no division, it is a unit. It has nothing to do with nature vs. nurture, because it is such a stupid question. We need both. We, the family, need a life, not a bunch of melodramatic Hollywood traditions, or crying sessions, because we didn't end up like a perfect family. Get real, kids and parents are the same thing … it's just size, and time. So if you want to be a good parent, be a good kid; and if you want to have good kids, be a good parent. As for friends, at times you cannot control them, but the bad ones will come up. If I were a parent, I will ask my children to trust their gut feeling. That way, they will develop independence, and will start to build their intuition, or as I like to call it, …the Holy Spirit.

Just remember to not misplace your heart, in the wrong places such as: greed, extra-marital affairs, abusive words, alcohol, lack of care and supervision, blackmailing friends who want your money, rapists, gangsters, mafias … you know, the obvious things that have been known to ruin families. My motto is, don't ask for trouble, get better at keeping it away. If you are a stressful parent, wrestle with your children (not BEAT THEM UP!!!). I am 99.9% sure, the stress will somehow lessen, according to how much you sweat. Take time to eat out, you will see other families there too, and realize, there are worse families around you.

Remember, to never compare. Do not think you are trash!! When your children did something bad, MAKE SURE THEY UNDERSTAND!! Tell your children, the importance of keeping each other, healthy and wise. They will have a better life, in the end. Have some confidence, you can do it!! My parents did, and they had three infamous children.

* = *Geotropism*

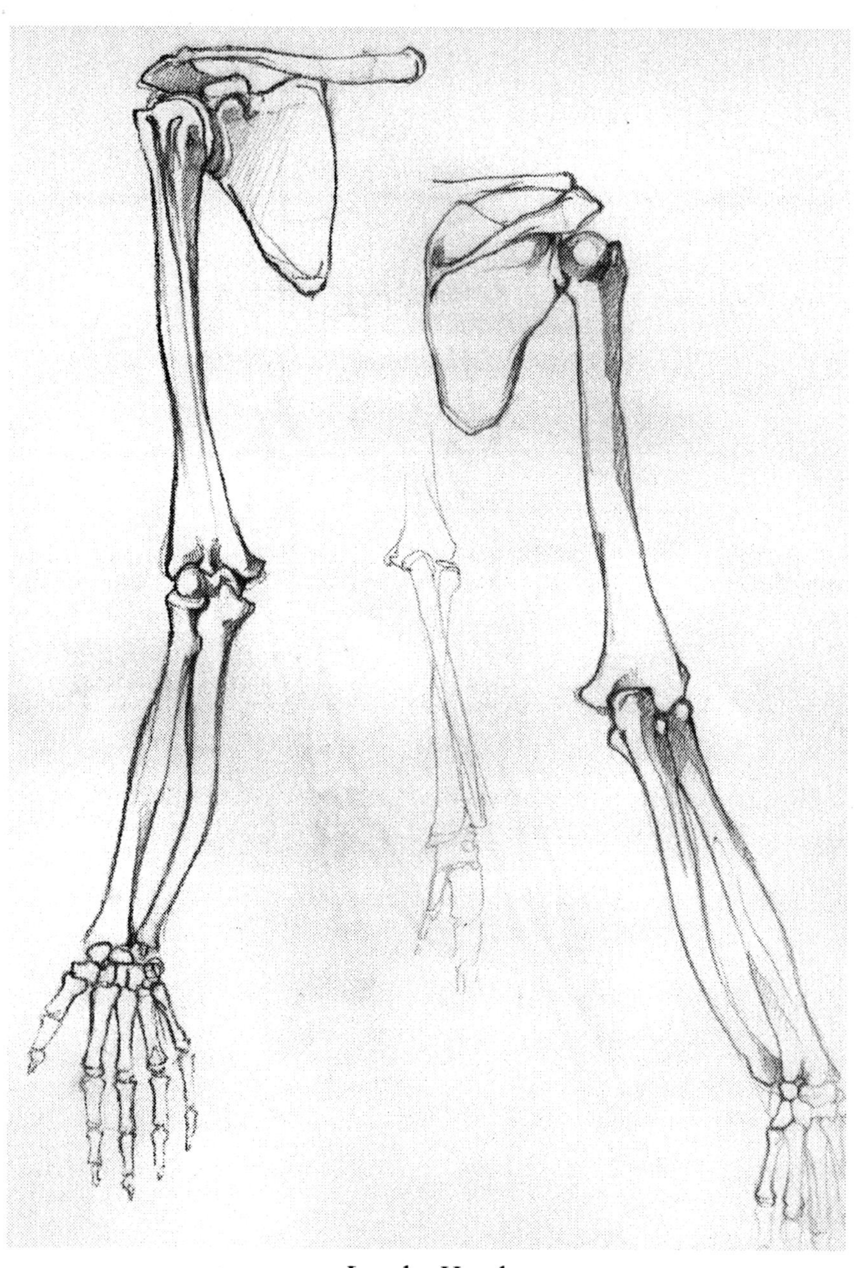

Lend a Hand

Your Thyroid Problem and Energy

Fiction by Diana Kurniawan

Have you been lacking energy to go to class? Feeling a lack of concentration, when studying or during lecture? Do you often want to stay on the couch, and sleep all day? Two things can cause these types of behaviors: senioritis, or *under-active thyroid problem.* Since there has never been such a thing as senioritis, then by system of elimination, under-active thyroid problem, may be the answer to your dilemma.

Under active thyroid, may cause many people to feel less energetic, and often make them feel more tired than usual, according to Health Magazine (1999). The thyroid, located below the Adam's apple, is the body's accelerator, controlling the tempo, of all internal processes, such as: heart beat, digestion, even thoughts. If the thyroid does not work hard enough, or if it works too hard, life will start to go haywire.

Many people, especially college students, whose lives contain mostly of work or school, and not much time for relaxation, are perfect targets for overwhelmed thyroid problems. Women are most vulnerable to this issue, and at least one in five, will develop a thyroid problem (and not even know it).

One can check the under active thyroid problem, by a simple blood test, that can spot malfunction thyroid in just several minutes. The normal age for thyroid problem is around 35, but there were several cases, where women had developed malfunctioning thyroid, much earlier than the age of 35 (*consult your local health practitioner*).

"Maybe, I am just getting older," is one of the many common remarks people concluded, when they come across symptoms, such as: depression, lack of energy, or loss of concentration. One may never know the dangers of lack of information.

Malfunctioning thyroid sufferers, may also gain an average of five 10 pounds, because their metabolism would slow down (*consult your health practitioner for the dangers of obesity, and depression*). There will also be an increase in cholesterol level, and an increase, in the risk of heart disease (*if exercise is a part of your daily regimen, you may run for it, and drink plenty of water*).

When women hit the age of 50, or even 60, thyroid diseases or disorders, climb sharply. It is better, to check at an early age, rather than find out later, at the age of 30 or 40, that there had been a severe thyroid malfunction. Therefore, check your thyroid, and catch this problem early, before your life goes haywire.

Let it out! Bad Air!

About the Author

Diana Kurniawan, MPH, a previously beautiful creature, now a part of the everyday society, and finally reached insanity. Her writing is, and has always been, from inspiration, or from the spin off, of life's satire and humor. She has a degree in Public Health, and is continuing her endeavor, in helping the community, and defending the planet. What you have just read, are spiritual speculations, because her interests, includes: reducing teen violence, decreasing teen pregnancies, and increasing public knowledge, of common health problems, in everyday situations. She is currently working on her novel, and she hopes to be discovered, by either Prince William of Windsor, his eldest cousin, Prince Peter Phillips, or the richest man on the earth. She is superwoman, in the making, but a little more, saucy. She serves as a volunteer, contributing freelancer, without the nice car, or the glitz. What a great heart, and great person she is.

Printed in the United States
41460LVS00007B/38

9 781420 862164